Pebble®
Plus

The U.S. Constitution

by Kathy Allen

Consulting Editor: Gail Saunders-Smith, PhD

Consultant: Philip Bigler
Director, The James Madison Center
Harrisonburg, Virginia

Capstone
press®

Mankato, Minnesota

Pebble Plus is published by Capstone Press,
151 Good Counsel Drive, P.O. Box 669, Mankato, Minnesota 56002.
www.capstonepress.com

1 2 3 4 5 6 11 10 09 08 07 06

Library of Congress Cataloging-in-Publication Data
Allen, Kathy.
    The U.S. Constitution / by Kathy Allen.
    p. cm.
    Includes bibliographical references and index.
    ISBN-13: 978-0-7368-9594-1 (hardcover)
    ISBN-10: 0-7368-9594-9 (hardcover)
    ISBN-13: 978-0-7368-9499-9 (softcover pbk.)
    ISBN-10: 0-7368-9499-3 (softcover pbk.)
    1. United States. Constitution—Juvenile literature. 2. Constitutional history—United States—Juvenile
literature. I. Title.
E303.A44 2007
342.7302'9—dc22   2006004142

Summary: Simple text and photographs introduce the U.S. Constitution, its history, and significance.

Editorial Credits
Martha E. H. Rustad, editor; Linda Clavel, designer; Deirdre Barton, photo researcher/photo editor

Photo Credits
Art Resource, NY/Christy Howard Chander, 12–13
Corbis/Francis G. Mayer, 6–7, 11 (left); Geoffrey Clements, 11 (right); Ariel Skelley, 20–21
Getty Images Inc./Todd Gipstein, cover
North Wind Picture Archives, 8–9
Photodisc, 1 (right); 15 (middle), 17
Shutterstock/Brandon Seidel, 1 (left); Scott Rothstein, 4–5; Manoj Valappil, 15 (left); bluestocking, 15 (right);
    Jason Maehl, 18–19

Note to Parents and Teachers

This book supports national standards related to power, authority, and governance. This
book describes and illustrates the U.S. Constitution. The images support early readers
in understanding the text. The repetition of words and phrases helps early readers learn
new words. This book also introduces early readers to subject-specific vocabulary words,
which are defined in the Glossary section. Early readers may need assistance to read
some words and to use the Table of Contents, Glossary, Read More, Internet Sites, and
Index sections of the book.

Table of Contents

What Is the Constitution?

The Constitution is
a document.
It is the basic law
of the United States.

Making the U.S. Constitution

The United States was created
after the Revolutionary War.
The country needed
a new government.

In 1787, the country's leaders met.

They worked all summer long to write the Constitution.

George Washington
led the meetings.
James Madison and
other leaders helped
write the Constitution.

George Washington

James Madison

A New Government

The U.S. Constitution

was finished

on September 17, 1787.

Thirty-nine leaders signed it.

The Constitution set up

the government.

It gave the government

three parts. Each part has

an equal amount of power.

The Constitution

President

Congress

Supreme Court

The Bill of Rights was added
to the Constitution in 1791.
It lists the rights that the
government cannot take away.

Today, people still must
follow the Constitution.
Courts make sure that
no laws go against it.

Supreme Court building

The Constitution keeps
our government fair.
It keeps Americans free.

Glossary

Bill of Rights—a list of ten amendments to the Constitution that protect your right to speak freely, to practice religion, and other important rights

document—a piece of paper containing important information

equal—the same as something else in size, value, or amount

government—the people and laws that rule a town, state, country, or other area

law—a rule made by the government that must be obeyed

Revolutionary War—the war in which the 13 American colonies won their independence from Great Britain; it lasted from 1775 to 1783.

right—something the law allows people to do, such as the right to vote or the right to speak freely; the government cannot take away our rights.

Read More

Catrow, David. *We the Kids: The Preamble to the Constitution of the United States.* New York: Dial Books for Young Readers, 2002.

Knox, Barbara. *George Washington.* Pebble Books: First Biographies. Mankato, Minn.: Capstone Press, 2004.

Welsbacher, Anne. *James Madison.* United States Presidents. Edina, Minn.: Abdo, 2002.

Internet Sites

FactHound offers a safe, fun way to find Internet sites related to this book. All of the sites on FactHound have been researched by our staff.

Here's how:

1. Visit *www.facthound.com*

2. Choose your grade level.

3. Type in this book ID **0736895949** for age-appropriate sites. You may also browse subjects by clicking on letters, or by clicking on pictures and words.

4. Click on the **Fetch It** button.

FactHound will fetch the best sites for you!

Index

Word Count: 138
Grade: 1
Early-Intervention Level: 15